23

NIGHT FLIERS
Moths in Your Backyard

Written by Nancy Loewen
Illustrated by Brandon Reibeling

Backyard Bugs

Thanks to our advisers for their expertise,
research, knowledge, and advice:

Gary A. Dunn, M.S., Director of Education
Young Entomologists' Society
Lansing, Michigan

Susan Kesselring, M.A., Literacy Educator
Rosemount-Apple Valley-Eagan (Minnesota) School District

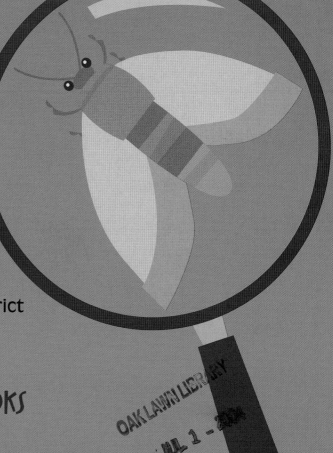

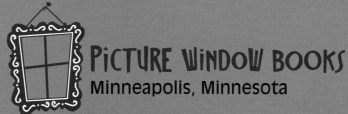
PICTURE WINDOW BOOKS
Minneapolis, Minnesota

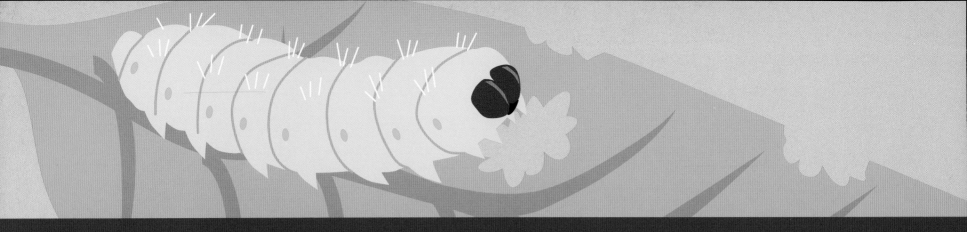

Managing Editor: Bob Temple
Creative Director: Terri Foley
Editors: Nadia Higgins, Brenda Haugen
Editorial Adviser: Andrea Cascardi
Copy Editor: Laurie Kahn
Designer: Melissa Voda
Page production: Picture Window Books
The illustrations in this book were prepared digitally.

Picture Window Books
5115 Excelsior Boulevard
Suite 232
Minneapolis, MN 55416
1-877-845-8392
www.picturewindowbooks.com

Printed in the United States of America.

Library of Congress Cataloging-in-Publication Data
Loewen, Nancy, 1964–
Night fliers : moths in your backyard / written by Nancy Loewen ; illustrated by Brandon
Reibeling.
p. cm. — (Backyard bugs)
Summary: Describes the physical characteristics, life cycle, and behavior of moths.
Includes bibliographical references (p.   ).
ISBN 1-4048-0144-8 (hardcover)
1. Moths Juvenile literature. [1. Moths.] I. Reibeling, Brandon, ill. II. Title.
QL544.2 .L67 2003
595.78—dc21
                                                                          2003006101

Table of Contents

Butterflies of the Night

At night, the yard becomes a different place. The grass feels cool on your toes. Fireflies blink here and there. Crickets chirp, and moths glide over flowers and flutter around porch lights. Moths are like butterflies of the night.

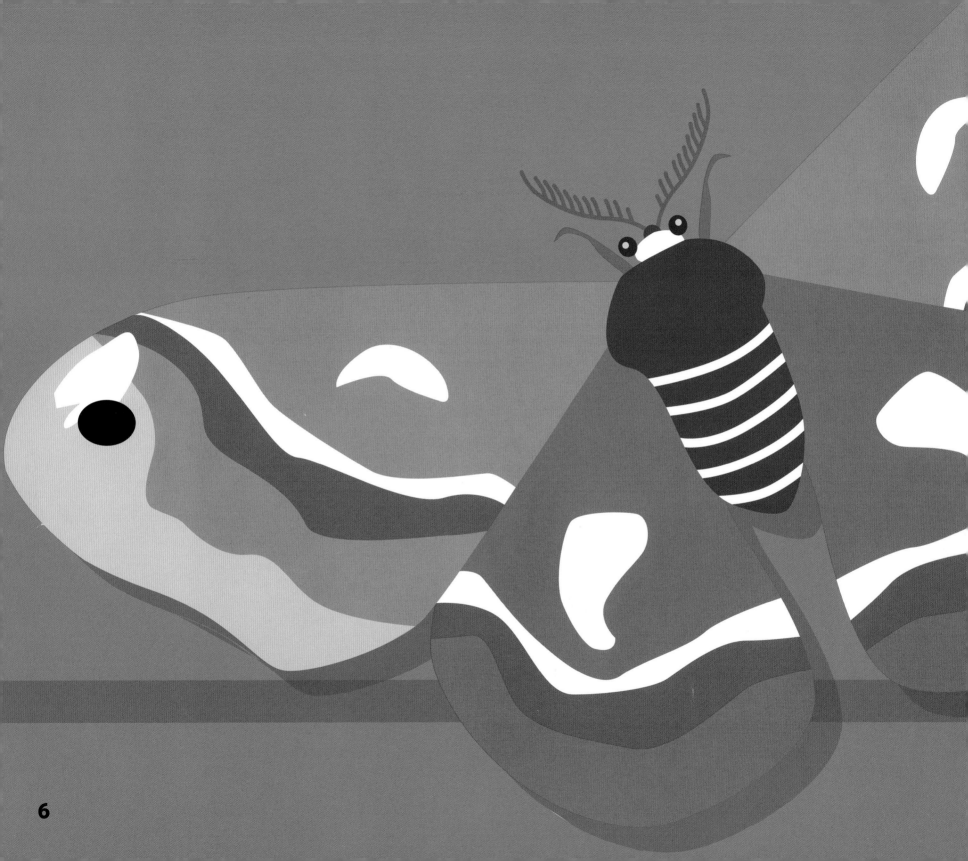

Like a butterfly, a moth has four wings covered with powder. The powder is made of tiny scales laid out like the shingles on a roof.

Moths also have antennae, or feelers, on their heads. The antennae help moths smell. They also help moths keep their balance.

Moths live all over the world, except in Antarctica. There are more than 200,000 kinds of moths, compared to 18,500 kinds of butterflies.

Blending In

Most moths aren't very colorful. Their wings are different shades of brown and gray. They blend in perfectly with tree bark, soil, or the undersides of leaves. That makes it difficult for their enemies to see them.

Moths are food for many animals, including bats, birds, lizards, spiders, and other insects.

But not all moths blend in. Over there—do you see the big pale-green moth? That's called a luna moth. It's as beautiful as any butterfly, don't you think?

Feeding on Flowers

Look over there by the flower bed. Is that a hummingbird?
No, it's a hawkmoth. It's also called a sphinx moth.
What do you think it's doing in those flowers?

That's right. It's eating! Some moths feed on nectar, a sweet
liquid found in flowers. Their mouths are long, thin tubes.

When a moth isn't feeding, its mouth is curled up, like a party noisemaker. When a moth wants to eat, it uncurls its mouth and sucks, as if it were drinking from a straw.

11

An Important Job

There it goes, off to another flower. As it eats, the moth is doing a very important job. It's helping plants make seeds.

Pollen is a special powder found in flowers. Plants need pollen from other plants in order to make seeds and bear fruit. When moths eat, pollen sticks to little hairs on their legs and is spread to other plants.

Moths taste with special hair on their feet.

13

Eggs, Caterpillars, and Cocoons

Look at a leaf. There might be a moth egg on it. Moth eggs look like little beads.

Moths lay eggs on the undersides of leaves. A female moth lays the eggs after she mates with a male. The eggs will hatch into caterpillars.

Male moths find female moths by smelling them with their antennae.

15

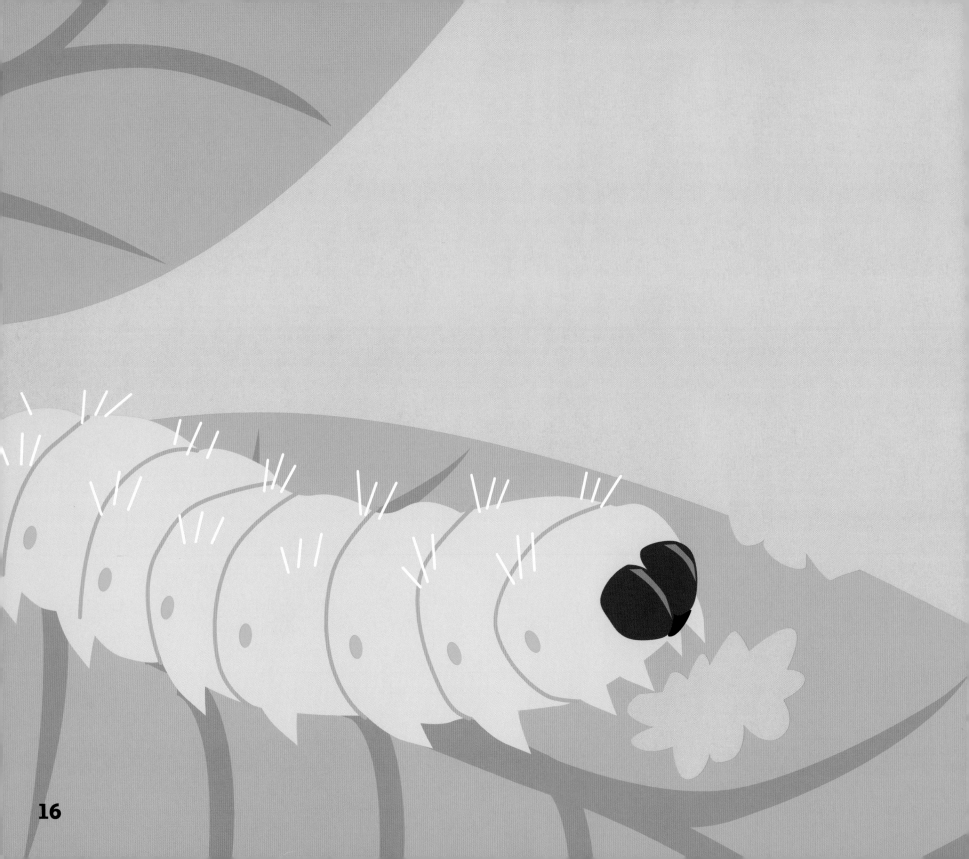

The first thing a new caterpillar does is eat its own eggshell! After that, it feeds on plants. It doesn't drink nectar like some adult moths do.

As the caterpillar grows, its armor-like covering gets too small. The covering cracks and breaks off. This is called molting. A new, bigger covering is underneath the old covering.

Some kinds of moths are considered pests. Their caterpillars can hurt crops and trees.

Do you see this little lump? It's called a cocoon. When a moth caterpillar is fully grown, it spins silk around its body.

Inside the cocoon, the caterpillar's body becomes soft and mushy. It now is called a pupa. The soft, mushy pupa turns into a new moth.

Many moths stay in the cocoon stage all winter. Others spend the winter as eggs or caterpillars.

Summer Evening Friends

Adult moths don't live long—usually just one or two weeks. But they are important parts of nature. Some help plants make seeds. Some are food for other living creatures.

What would a summer evening be without them?

Look Closely at a Moth and a Butterfly

Wings—When at rest, a moth folds its wings over its back. A butterfly holds them upright. Moths usually have less colorful wings than butterflies.

Antennae—Moths don't have knobs at the end of their antennae, but butterflies do. In some kinds of moths, the antennae can be very large, with many branches.

Body—Moths usually have thicker, hairier bodies than butterflies have.

The easiest way to tell a moth apart from a butterfly is to pay attention to *when* you see one. Most butterflies are active during the day, while most moths are active at night.

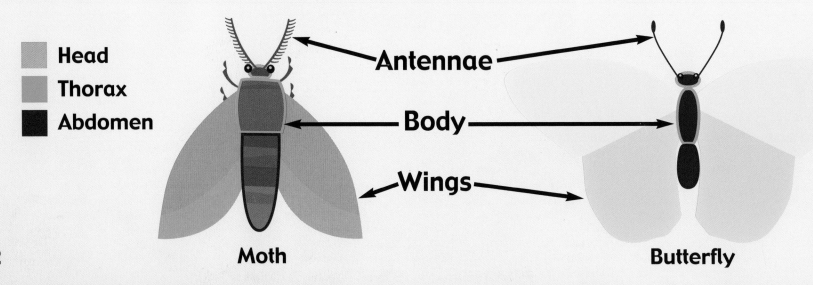

Head
Thorax
Abdomen
Antennae
Body
Wings
Moth
Butterfly

Fun Facts

- Some moths' wings have markings that look like eyes. The markings make the moths seem much bigger than they are. This scares off the moths' enemies.

- Scientists don't really know why moths flutter around lights. Some scientists think moths aren't really attracted to light. They believe the light confuses the moths.

- Silk cloth comes from the cocoons of silk caterpillars. They live in Asia. When a cocoon is unraveled, the silk thread can be more than 2,000 feet (610 meters) long!

- Moths sometimes feed on rotted fruit or tree sap.

- Some male moths have big, feathery antennae that let them smell and find females more than three miles (five kilometers) away!

Make a Moth

For your next art project, why not make a moth? All you need is dark-colored paper (black, brown, or gray), glue, and flour.

Use the glue to draw a moth shape on the paper. You can fill in the wings completely with glue or make patterns. Next, sprinkle flour all over the glue. Shake the extra flour off the paper, and your moth appears! You can cut it out when it dries.

You also can try making a bunch of moths with different colors of paper. Put the moths you make on the ground, against a tree, or on a plant. How well do they show up?

Words to Know

antennae–Antennae (an-TEN-ee) are feelers on an insect's head. Antennae is the word for more than one antenna (an-TEN-uh).

mate–Male and female moths mate by joining together special parts of their bodies. After they've mated, the female can lay eggs.

nectar–Nectar is a sweet liquid that comes from flowers.

pollen–Pollen is a special powder found in flowers. Plants need pollen from other plants to make seeds and bear fruit.

sap–Sap is a liquid that flows through plants.

silk–Silk is long, thin threads that stick together to make a cocoon.

To Learn More

At the Library

Arnosky, Jim. *Crinkleroot's Guide to Knowing Butterflies & Moths.* New York: Simon & Schuster Books for Young Readers, 1996.

Brimner, Larry Dane. *Butterflies and Moths.* New York: Children's Press, 1999.

Frost, Helen. *Moths.* Mankato, Minn.: Pebble Books, 2001.

McEvey, Shane F. *Moths and Butterflies.* Philadelphia: Chelsea House Publishers, 2001.

On the Web

enature.com
http://www.enature.com/guides/select_Insects_and_Spiders.asp
Articles about and photos of almost 300 species of insects and spiders

The National Park Service
http://www1.nature.nps.gov/wv/insects.htm
A guide to finding and studying insects at national parks

University of Kentucky Department of Entomology
http://www.uky.edu/Agriculture/Entomology/ythfacts/entyouth.htm
A kid-friendly site with insect games, jokes, articles, and resources

Fact Hound
Fact Hound offers a safe, fun way to find Web sites related to this book. All of the sites on Fact Hound have been researched by our staff.
http://www.facthound.com

1. Visit the Fact Hound home page.
2. Enter a search word related to this book, or type in this special code: 1404801448.
3. Click on the FETCH IT button.

Your trusty Fact Hound will fetch the best sites for you!

Index

The Twelve
Dancing Princesses

The Twelve
Dancing Princesses

Jane Ray
after the brothers Grimm

ORCHARD BOOKS

for my sisters Elizabeth and Caroline, with much love

ORCHARD BOOKS
96 Leonard Street, London EC2A 4XD
Orchard Books Australia
Unit 31/56 O'Riordan Street, Alexandria, NSW 2015
ISBN 1 85213 997 8 (hardback)
ISBN 1 84121 778 6 (paperback)
First published in Great Britain in 1996
This edition published in 2002
Illustrations © Jane Ray 1996
The right of Jane Ray to be identified as the illustrator of this
work has been asserted by her in accordance with the
Copyright, Designs and Patents Act, 1988.
A CIP catalogue record for this book is available from the British Library.
1 3 5 7 9 10 8 6 4 2 (hardback)
3 5 7 9 10 8 6 4 2 (paperback)
Printed in Belgium

There was once a king who had twelve daughters, each one as clever and beautiful as the next. He loved them all dearly but was puzzled by a mystery that happened night after night.

Every evening the king would tenderly kiss his daughters and settle them down to sleep in the long bedchamber they shared. He then tiptoed out, always taking care to lock and bolt the door behind him.

Yet every morning the princesses were tired and wan and their silken shoes were danced to pieces. Where did they go each night? And how did they leave their room? The king was determined to solve the mystery. For one thing twelve new pairs of dancing slippers a day was costing him a fortune.

The princesses were certainly not telling, so the king issued a proclamation. Any man who could discover their secret would marry one of the princesses and rule the kingdom with her on the old king's death. But he must find the answer in three days and three nights or be banished from the kingdom forever.

Marry one of the beautiful princesses and become king! You can imagine that it wasn't long before most of the young men in the kingdom were queueing up at the palace gates to try their luck.

The first to try was the son of a king. He was led to a small dressing room next to the princesses' bedchamber. He was enchanted by the twelve young women and when the eldest offered him a cup of sweet wine he happily drank it. Then, when the princesses had gone to their room, he checked that their bedroom door had been left ajar and settled down to his night-long vigil. But, however hard he struggled, the prince could not keep his eyes open. He was

overcome by sleep and suddenly it was morning. There in their beds were the
twelve princesses, sleeping soundly, and there on the floor were the twelve
pairs of worn-out slippers, the evidence of his failure.

The second night, the same sweet wine, the same overwhelming need to
sleep and the same failure. And again the third night. The young prince was
duly banished from the kingdom and another suitor took up the challenge.

And so it continued. The king was in despair. Were his daughters able to
outwit every man in the kingdom?

Some time later a poor soldier, returning wounded from a battle in a faraway country, sat down to rest by the side of the road. He was enjoying his simple meal of bread and cheese when an old woman approached and, because the soldier was a kind man, he offered her half his lunch.

"Where are you heading?" the old woman asked. The soldier laughed. "Off to try my luck at the palace", he said. "I could quite fancy being king!"

But the old woman remained serious. "Don't touch the wine those clever girls offer you. Just pretend to drink, then pretend to fall asleep. And if you wear this cloak, you'll become invisible and be able to follow them wherever they go."

The soldier was puzzled, but he thanked the strange old woman, took the cloak, and set off for the palace.

By now the king had given up hope of solving his daughters' secret, but he greeted the soldier courteously. And so, when bedtime came, the soldier was led to the small room next to the princesses' bedchamber. The eldest princess offered him a cup of wine and the soldier pretended to sip... and to sip some more. The wine did not run down his throat but into a small sponge he had cleverly tied under his chin.

Then, as if overcome with tiredness, the soldier yawned loudly and rolled over onto his bed. "Silly fool," said the eldest princess. And laughing merrily, the twelve sisters danced into their room to prepare for the night ahead.

They flung open their cupboards and trunks and began to dress themselves in fine lace and linen, embroidered silk and rich velvet and brocade. They curled and plaited each other's hair, painted lips and powdered faces, ruffled fans and finally every princess slipped on a new pair of dancing shoes . . .

Only the youngest could not enjoy herself. "Something feels wrong tonight,"
she said. But her eldest sister – impatient to be off – told her not to be a silly
goose, and clapped her hands three times. A door appeared in the wall and
slowly swung open and the twelve princesses disappeared.

The soldier clambered from his bed and hurried after them, flinging his magic cloak around his shoulders as he went. But in his haste he stumbled on his wounded leg and stepped on the hem of the youngest princess' dress. "What was that?" she cried. "Someone is following us. I know something's not right tonight."

"Nonsense," said her eldest sister. But the youngest sensed something all the same and kept glancing over her shoulder, as they made their way down flights of stairs and along corridors. Finally they arrived at a small wooden door. This opened out onto a garden.

The soldier drew his breath: he had never seen such a magical place.

The princesses hurried through the silvery trees, which glimmered in the moonlight.

They came to a garden of gold, where plump and delicious fruits hung down from the branches, burnished and bronzed. Then they stepped through an arch of roses into a third garden all of diamonds which sparkled and shimmered in the dark like a spangled sky of stars.

In each garden the soldier felt he must be dreaming and reached up to snap off a twig, just to be sure. Each time the youngest princess was startled by the noise; and each time her sisters laughed away her fears and hurried her on.

An avenue of diamond-studded trees led down to a lake and there, on
the water, bobbed twelve little painted boats. In each sat a handsome prince,
waiting to row the princesses across the water.

The soldier, growing used to this strange and magical world by now,
climbed into the boat with the youngest princess, taking care to cover himself
completely with his invisible cloak.

After a while the little prince rowing the boat stopped to rest. "Why is the boat so slow tonight, when I'm rowing as hard as I always do?" The youngest sister only shivered in reply.

Across the lake stood a wonderful castle. Lights shone from every window, fireworks exploded in the sky above, and the sound of drums and trumpets, flutes and violins reached down to the boats, urging all to join the party.

The princesses ran up to the castle and danced with their princes all through the night. They ate the most mouthwatering of foods and drank the finest wines. The soldier, hidden safely in his cloak, danced alone, weaving amongst the couples and stealing morsels of food from under the noses of the unseeing guests. Once, feeling very bold, he took a sip from the youngest princess' goblet.

"Now someone is helping themselves to my drink," she said, almost in tears. But her eldest sister, whirling past, only laughed at her. "Oh do stop worrying and come and dance. We've only a few hours left."

And sure enough, their slippers were soon so worn through that they could not be danced in a minute longer. It was time for the princesses to go home.

The princes rowed the sisters back across the lake and this time the soldier travelled with the eldest princess. All the young women were beautiful in their own ways, but she was the most interesting to him.

The princesses promised to meet their princes the following night, and hurried back through the three gardens and along the palace passageways.

They were tiring by now, and sleepily climbed the last flight of stairs. The soldier slipped past them in his cloak. And by the time the princesses peeped in through his door he was lying in his bed, apparently fast asleep and snoring gently.

"Silly fool!" yawned the eldest princess. "But our secret is still safe." And she lingered a moment, watching him as he slept.

The next morning the soldier felt sure it had all been a dream, in spite of the three twigs he had picked from the gardens. He decided to keep his vigil once more before seeing the king. The second night was exactly like the first and the soldier enjoyed himself so much he couldn't resist following the princesses for a third night of dancing and feasting. This last time he came away with a golden goblet under his cloak as further proof.

On the fourth morning, the king wearily summoned the soldier to his study. The sisters hid outside the door to hear how he would fare. "Have you discovered how my daughters wear out their slippers every night?" asked the king.

"I have, your majesty," replied the soldier. "They dance away the night in an underground castle, with twelve handsome princes." And he produced from his pockets the three twigs and the golden goblet, as he explained about the hidden door, the three gardens, the lake and the castle.

The king called for each of his daughters in turn and, beginning with the youngest, asked whether the soldier's story was true. Each princess hung her head in silence until the eldest one spoke. "Father, it's true," she replied. "The soldier has outwitted us."

"Then you must decide which of my daughters you wish to marry," said the king. The soldier knew that he had already chosen the eldest. She saw that the soldier was kind as well as clever, and was pleased to accept. "Just provided," she said with a smile, "that we can have plenty of dancing at the wedding."

The wedding took place soon afterwards and they danced the night away.

When, some time later, the old king died, the princess and
the soldier ruled the kingdom together fairly and happily
for many years.

And, as queen, the eldest sister decreed that she and her
sisters should go dancing as often and as late into the night as
they wished, and she appointed a royal shoemaker to keep
their dancing shoes in good repair.